THINK MORTALLY

A SURVIVAL GUIDE FOR YOUNG ADULTS

JOSEPH BERGER

ILLUSTRATED BY ANDRIY SLOBODIANYK

Also By

BERGERAC PUBLISHING, LLC

NONFICTION

Calm Outside

Football Frenzy

CHILDRENS

Pour Nimbus

BERGERAC CLASSICS - Modernized

Resurrection by Leo Tolstoy

The Call of the Wild by Jack London

The Life and Adventures of Robinson Crusoe by Daniel Defoe

for

B. Ryan Teller

who turned many bad decisions

into a surprisingly educational franchise

CONTENTS

INTRODUCTION

 *"An ounce of prevention is worth a pound of cure."*

BENJAMIN FRANKLIN

Congratulations, young adults! You've survived the gauntlet of childhood - illness, falls, scrapes, sports, swimming lessons, acne, the horrors of high school and perhaps a pandemic. In conquering these challenges, you've had your own personal superheroes - your parents and caregivers. Like vigilant guardians, they shielded you, shepherded you, buckled you up, caught you when you stumbled, and guided you safely through life's early stages.

However, there's a catch. While navigating the perils of infancy to adolescence, you may have missed a few crucial life lessons along the way. Unfortunately, as you transition into adulthood, the number of harmful and potentially life-altering situations increases exponentially. These situations could shame, injure, disable, bankrupt, or even kill you.

The statistics are sobering. According to the National Safety Council, preventable injuries and deaths among young adults have doubled per capita in the last 30 years. Each year, there are nearly 21 million preventable injuries and over 225,000 preventable deaths in the United States alone.

But here's the good news: learning how to prevent these tragedies doesn't have to be a dry and boring exercise. In this humorous, slightly irreverent, yet undeniably practical book, I'll combine legitimate self-defense tips with a healthy dose of laughter to ease your transition into adulthood. My focus will be on a blend of proven, anecdotal, and common-sense advice for keeping you safe. Through witty anecdotes, ridiculous scenarios, and a dash of sarcasm, I'll arm you with the valuable knowledge you need to avoid life's most embarrassing "oops" moments.

This guide sorts modern life into its most hazardous habitats —each chapter a field manual for a different environment of risk. Inside, you'll learn how to handle everyday missions safely while avoiding unnecessary injury, humiliation, or death. Comprehensive? Pretty close. Useful? Hopefully—if you actually read it!

So, without further ado, let's dive in for some laughs, caution, a healthy dose of facepalms, and the skills to truly survive!

CHAPTER ONE

RISE AND SHINE

> *"My bed and I are perfect for each other, but my alarm clock keeps trying to break us up."*

ANONYMOUS

I hope you're getting a good night's sleep. We'll address that. Also, a lot of dangerous stuff can happen when you're sleeping that is beyond your control, as early man figured out. How great are doors? Let's focus on things you can do to prevent injury or death until you wake up.

Your Goal: Cheat Sleep
The Risks: Physical and Mental Health Problems; Brain Fog; Poor Performance

THE LESSON: SLEEP LIKE A BOSS

Common Mistakes: Trading precious sleep for late-night Netflix binges, demanding work schedules, or simply poor sleep hygiene – we've all done it. Your sleep bank is just like your money bank. You can't keep withdrawing without making deposits or you'll go broke. Be on the lookout for those telltale signs of sleep deprivation: constant yawning, TV-induced dozing, morning grogginess, foggy brain, and mood swings. If you're experiencing these symptoms despite getting eight hours of shuteye, consider other factors like sleep apnea, caffeine intake, or alcohol consumption. The Centers for Disease Control and Prevention (CDC) has even declared insufficient sleep a "public health problem," costing the US a whopping $411 billion annually. It's a problem that affects everyone, so let's talk about how to conquer it.

Recommended Approach: Forget naps, energy drinks, and pushing through exhaustion. The key to healthy sleep habits is prioritizing quantity and quality rest. Here's your roadmap to restful nights:

- Develop a Routine: Just like brushing your teeth, establish a regular bedtime routine that signals to your body it's time to wind down. This could include reading, stretching, changing into comfy pajamas, and brushing your teeth.
- Consistency is Key: Stick to a consistent sleep schedule, including weekends. This helps regulate your body's natural sleep-wake cycle.
- Banish the Screens: Banish televisions and screen time from your bedroom. The blue light emitted from electronic devices is known to disrupt sleep patterns.
- Protect Your Time: Guard your sleep time fiercely. Don't let social obligations or work commitments encroach on this essential self-care too regularly.
- Gradual Change: Start by going to bed just 15 minutes earlier each night, gradually increasing the time until 7 to 8 hours becomes your new normal.
- Embrace the Light: Maximize exposure to natural light during the day. Wake up with the sunrise to feel more tired at night – it's a natural sleep aid.

These initial changes might be tough, but stick with them! Remember, prioritizing sleep isn't just about feeling rested in the morning – it's an investment in your overall health and well-being. Trust me, once you experience the benefits of quality sleep, it'll be a game-changer for your mental health and overall well-being.

Your Goal: Phone Charging
The Risk: Electrical Shock; Fire Hazard; The Dreaded
Dead Morning Phone

THE LESSON: POWER UP SAFELY

Common Mistakes: Ah, the panic of a phone battery
teetering on the edge of oblivion, just before you connect it to
that trusty (but maybe a little worse for wear) charging cable.
Smartphone chargers, especially those in the bedroom, endure

a lot of wear and tear. Over time, that plastic coating splits and frays, exposing those delicate wires within. Don't ignore it and hope for the best— manufacturers covered those wires for a reason!

Recommended Approach: Before you shell out for a new charger, consider a simple DIY fix. Grab some black electrical tape (the kind with "electrical" in the name is key!) and your trusty scissors. Wrap the exposed area securely, ensuring all those wires are tucked back into their protective casing. This quick fix can save you a few bucks.

Feeling adventurous? Treat yourself to a new, sturdier cable. Go wild and pick a vibrant color! And why not splurge on a longer one? Ten feet might sound excessive, but it'll free you from the shackles of charging your phone on the floor.

Celebrating a birthday soon? Hint to your loved ones about the wonders of wireless charging! A basic ten-watt charging pad is perfect for the bedroom. With eight hours to juice up your phone (see the previous chapter!), there's no risk of over-heating. Plus, opting for a larger pad means no more fiddling around trying to find that sweet spot.

If bedside notifications have you waking up at 2:30 AM with FOMO, consider a charging stand. You see alerts clearly while your phone charges, keeping you connected without sacrificing sleep. So, ditch the frayed cables and embrace the future of battery bliss. Your phone will thank you for it!

Your Goal: Creating a Vibe
The Risk: Burning Yourself or Others Alive

THE LESSON: DITCH THE CANDLES "LIT"-ERALLY!

Common Mistakes: Candle lovers, this one's for you. If you find yourself constantly lured by those tempting candle promotions, leading to a bedroom filled with flickering flames, let's talk safety. While candles offer a warm ambiance, remember, they're meant to be extinguished. Since the days of cave-dwelling humans, fire has been a comforting presence. But let's face it, we humans are pretty deep sleepers and unlike those caves, our bedrooms are considerably more flammable. How often do you toss, turn, and maybe even karate kick in your sleep? You get the picture. It's no surprise that candles are responsible for over 24,000 fires annually.

Recommended Approach: No need to completely abandon your love for mood lighting! Consider safer alternatives like battery-powered candles, many of which even flicker realistically (who knew?). Other options include:

- Low-lumen bulbs: Swap out your table lamp's bulb for a low-lumen option, creating a gentle glow.
- Peaceful TV moments: Put on something calming on your smart TV, dimming the screen brightness for a soothing effect.

"But I love the scent of candles!" you might say. Fear not, fellow aromatherapy enthusiast! While candles have provided delightful aromas for centuries, essential oils offer a safer and more efficient alternative. Try placing a few drops on a cotton ball and resting it on your pillow. Lavender, for example, is known to reduce anxiety and promote sleep, but ultimately, follow your nose and choose scents you find calming.

Diffusers are another fantastic option. Bamboo reed diffusers are both effective and affordable. With hundreds of scents available, the possibilities are endless. However, I recommend starting simple with single-note fragrances like tree or flower scents. My personal favorite? Hinoki oil (Japanese cypress), a truly grounding aroma.

By exploring these safer alternatives, you can continue to enjoy the benefits of mood lighting and aromatherapy while keeping your bedroom a safe haven.

Your Goal: Bed Nesting
The Risk: Asphyxiation; Suffocation; Strangulation

THE LESSON: CLEAR THE CLUTTER

Common Mistakes: Ah, the beloved bed. It's our refuge, our sanctuary, and unfortunately, sometimes a dumping ground for everything from clothes and backpacks to towels and stuffed animals. While it's tempting to dive into this cozy foxhole surrounded by your belongings, remember, clutter can be dangerous. In fact, suffocation is the fourth leading cause of preventable death.

Let's face it, you're most vulnerable when you're sleeping, especially if exhaustion or other factors are at play. So, before you drift off to dreamland, clear the bed of anything that could obstruct your breathing or entangle you. This includes your ever-growing mountain of pillows, that stray towel from your shower, and yes, even your teddy bear collection (sorry, but their love can be suffocating!).

Recommended Approach: Clear the clutter in your bedroom and claim your bed as safe zone.

- Embrace organization: Organize your belongings. Get some stackable bins (think milk cartons, but nicer) to separate your clean and dirty clothes. Invest in a large laundry bag for those clothes you can't bear to part with just yet.
- Downsize the pillows: Limit yourself to two pillows per person. Yes, you heard that right. Let go of the excessive pillow fort. It's time to embrace minimalism!
- Ditch the throw pillows: Most throw pillows are synthetic, dense, and harbor harmful flame-retardant chemicals called PBDEs. Not exactly the snuggle buddy you're looking for.
- Weighted blanket heaven: Seeking the ultimate hugger? Look no further than a weighted blanket. They come in many sizes, and price points, so there's one for every budget. Aim for a blanket between 12 and 15 pounds for maximum comfort. As an added bonus, it generally stays in place, providing that full-body hug you crave all night. You might even want to give it a name—oh yeah, you'll name it!

By clearing the clutter and embracing the weighted blanket hug, you're not only creating a safer sleep environment but also treating yourself to a more luxurious slumber experience. So, let's make our beds havens of comfort and safety, not death traps of pillows and stuffed animals. Sweet dreams!

CHAPTER TWO
PERILOUS PRIVY

ANONYMOUS

Deep within every home lies a chamber of mystery and mild danger: the bathroom. Observe the human—barefoot, half-awake, and surrounded by wet porcelain. Here they perform delicate rituals involving heat, water, and spinning blades. Remarkably, most survive.

Your Goal: First Pee Catch-Up
The Risk: Falls; Head Injury; Dead Legs, Relationship Issues

THE LESSON: TOILET TIME TIPS

Common Mistakes: Multitasking gurus, listen up! Trying to tackle your bathroom routine one-handed while glued to your phone is more likely to lead to messy chaos than efficiency. Let's face it, guys, we don't need to be juggling our devices with sleepy eyes. Dropped phones, near-toilet splashes, head-to-shelf collisions, and epic falls are all too common consequences of bathroom multitasking. And let's not forget the lost time spent scrolling through social media while perched on the throne. This "toilet time" marathon can wreak havoc on your circulation, nerves, and muscle control, not to mention your schedule.

Recommended Approach: Mom was right all along, guys. It's time to take a seat. If nature's calling urgently, standing is simply messy and hazardous. Wait it out or pinch it, but for the love of hygiene, don't attempt a balancing act with your pants down. And to those who scoff at the idea of "sitting like a girl," here's a newsflash: your toothbrush is probably within the splash perimeter. Take a break, rest your weary legs, and make your female roommates and family members proud!

Now, let's address the issue of time. Everyone, regardless of gender, should limit their toilet time to less than fifteen minutes. Why? Because that's the average time it takes for legs and feet to "fall asleep" while sitting, leading to wobbly legs and potential falls when you attempt to stand.

Here's another game-changer for your bathroom experience: invest in a bidet attachment! For less than a hundred bucks, you'll experience a cleaner feeling, use less toilet paper, and possibly even skip a few steps on your journey toward personal enlightenment. Trust me, it's worth the investment.

As for the phone, well, I won't say "put it down" because I know that's asking for a miracle. Instead, please keep sanitizing wipes handy and give your phone a thorough wipe-down after your bathroom session. Just remember, the key is dwelling time—the longer the disinfectant stays on the phone, the more effective it is.

So, guys, let's ditch the multitasking myths and embrace a more civilized and hygienic approach to the throne. Peasants stand—Knights sit. Now, go forth and conquer the porcelain throne with confidence!

Your Goal: Attack Morning Mouth
The Risk: Poisoning; Staining; Making a Bad Impression

THE LESSON: DETOX YOUR BATHROOM

Common Mistakes: We all do it - slather chemicals on our bodies and then rinse them down the drain, all while surrounded by a veritable cocktail of cleaning products. From toothpaste to bleach, the average bathroom houses a mini-hazardous waste site. And the numbers are alarming: calls to poison centers related to cleaning products and disinfectants have skyrocketed 149% since 2020!

The problem? We often leave bottles open, caps loose, and pumps un-clicked. This allows harmful gases and tiny particles to float around, turning our bathrooms into airborne toxin chambers. And don't get me started on the virtually identical pump bottles holding face wash and skin lotion— I need more clarity at 6 am!

Recommended Approach: Let's reclaim our bathrooms and transform them from chemical dumps into safe havens. Here's how:

- Toothbrush Turnaround: Replace your toothbrush every month. No exceptions!
- The Great Purge: Conduct a ruthless inventory. Toss expired products, those 2017 stocking stuffers you never used, and anything left behind by long-gone roommates. Imagine you're packing for a trip and only keep what you truly need. Everything else goes in the trash.
- Chemical Containment: Secure the lids and nozzles of all cleaning products and stash them in a bucket in a well-ventilated hall closet.
- Prescription Precision: Take medications as directed and discard expired ones responsibly (don't flush them!). Only take meds prescribed to you – experimenting with others can have serious consequences.
- Date Night Detox: Let's be honest, your date might be tempted to peek into your medicine cabinet, seeking clues about your personality. So, clean it up! Use it to set the stage and create the desired impression. What story do you want it to tell?

By making these simple changes, we can transform our bathrooms from hazardous zones into clean, safe havens. A little organization and awareness go a long way towards protecting our health and well-being.

Your Goal: Showering
The Risk: Falls; Burns; Illness; Asthma Exacerbation

THE LESSON: BLACK & GREEN AIN'T CLEAN

Common Mistakes: Stepping into the shower, feeling refreshed and ready for a clean start? Think again! While we often view showers as purifying, life restoring rituals, the reality can be quite different. A shocking 20% of all fatal and near-fatal home falls happen right there in the slippery confines of the shower stall. So, watch your footing and stay aware - it's literally a matter of life and limb!

But the danger doesn't stop there. Showers are also breeding grounds for germs, despite our reliance on hot water for cleansing. Don't let the steam fool you— soap, time, and friction are the real heroes in the fight against bacteria. In fact, water alone, even at scalding hot temperatures, would be ineffective against most germs and would only leave you with painful burns. So, while hot showers offer comfort, they also dry out your skin and create the perfect environment for bacteria and mold to flourish. Enter black mold, the notorious shower villain. This unwelcome guest can thrive in damp conditions, multiplying rapidly within 24 to 48 hours. For those with allergies or asthma, black mold is a nightmare, triggering runny noses, coughs, and itchy throats.

Recommended Approach: Ready to transform your shower from a germ-infested trap to a sparkling sanctuary? Here's how:

- Step Up Your Footing: Invest in a non-slip shower mat or those adorable little stickers, especially if your shower floor resembles an ice rink. If possible, consider installing a grab bar for added stability.
- Cleanse the Petri Dish: Ditch the idea that hot water magically sanitizes everything. Instead, embrace the power of a daily spray cleaner. Before you hop in, give the walls and shower curtain a quick spritz. Don't forget to scrub them regularly for a deeper clean. Repeat the process after you shower to keep germs at bay.
- Loofah Love: Don't let your trusty loofah become a haven for bacteria. Wash it weekly to ensure it's clean and ready for action.

- Showerhead Shine: Give your showerhead some much-needed TLC. Fill a gallon-sized zip-lock bag with vinegar and submerge the showerhead (screw it off or secure it with a rubber band) for 2-3 hours. This vinegar bath will kill bacteria lurking in the nozzles and eliminate pesky hard water deposits.

With these simple steps, you can transform your shower from a germ-infested battleground into a safe and refreshing haven. Breathe deeply, relax, and enjoy the shower experience without worries!

CHAPTER THREE

HELL'S A KITCHEN

"Recipes should include pictures of the mess you have to clean up after!"

QUOTEMENT

You're spending more time unbagging, unwrapping, and reheating meals than actual cooking. No judgment. You'll discover the joy of cooking and eating fresh food, eventually. For now, let's go over some basic stuff that will help keep you alive in the kitchen until that time.

Your Goal: Making Toast
The Risk: Electrocution; Fire; Smoke

THE LESSON: TOAST BREAD NOT ORGANS

Common Mistakes: Ah, the golden brown delights of toasted bread, bagels, muffins, and even the occasional toaster waffle! But what happens when your food gets stuck, refusing to budge from the fiery depths of your toaster? Do you reach for the closest tool at hand, perhaps a trusty butter knife? Well, this situation was the original inspiration for *Think Mortally*. Yes, one of my sons (not to be named) was going in hot. Stop!

While you may have been a champion at "Operation" back in the day, attempting to pry out toast with a metal object is not a game. It's a recipe for disaster, with the potential for painful shocks and even cardiac arrest. Remember, statistics say that half of all home electrocutions are fatal, claiming four lives every week. Those are some scary odds!

Recommended Approach: Don't risk another toaster casualty. Here's how to safely retrieve your breaded delights without becoming an electrical conductor:

- Unplug it: This is the golden rule of toaster safety. Before you do anything else, reach back and disconnect the power cord. Now you can avoid any electrical jolts.
- Operation Trampoline: Unleash your inner child! Play around with the toaster levers, seeing if you can catapult your toast high enough to land safely in your waiting hands. Bonus points for mid-air catches!
- Utensil Savvy: If the trampoline trick doesn't work, remember to keep safety first. Use wooden chopsticks, plastic utensils, or anything non-conductive to retrieve your toast. These heroes will prevent your body from becoming part of the electrical circuit, keeping you safe and your hair flat.
- Prevention is Key: Plan ahead and avoid toast-related mishaps. Squish your bagel before toasting, flatten those muffin crevices, and turn bread short-end down. These simple steps won't affect the deliciousness of your food but will significantly reduce the chances of getting stuck.

Remember, a bit of preparation and awareness go a long way towards a safe and enjoyable toast-eating experience. So, ditch the risky knife, embrace safe retrieval techniques, and enjoy your toast to the fullest, shock-free!

Your Goal: Raiding the Fridge
The Risk: Poisoning; Retching; Blowing Eye Blood Vessels

THE LESSON: DON'T EAT SPOILED FOOD

Common Mistakes: We've all been there— famished and diving headfirst into the fridge, devouring whatever catches our eye. But before you take a bite of that Kung Pao chicken from last week or yogurt with a "best-by" date that screams November 2022, think again! Food poisoning is a real threat, affecting millions of Americans each year and sending hundreds of thousands to the hospital. With symptoms that mimic the flu but can feel like an eternity (24-48 hours to be exact), food poisoning is no laughing matter.

Recommended Approach: To avoid a date with food-borne illness, steer clear of these culprits:

- Spoiled Eggs, Meat, Seafood, and Leftovers: Freshness is key! When it comes to meat and seafood, trust your nose. Gray food? No way! And if something smells fishy—literally— it's probably not fit to eat. For eggs, a simple test will do. Drop it in a bowl of water – if it floats, it's bad!
- Leftovers: Don't let your leftovers linger. Chill them within an hour of eating to enjoy for up to five days max.
- Steak Lovers Rejoice: If you prefer your steak rare, breathe easy. Bacteria primarily reside on the surface, which gets cooked off during searing.
- Best-by Dates: Don't confuse these with expiration dates! They simply indicate the manufacturer's peak quality prediction. Only baby formula comes with a genuine expiration date. So, trust your nose – if it smells good, it probably is.
- Weekly Fridge Cleanse: Feeling overwhelmed by the fridge's contents? Implement a weekly cleaning ritual on trash day. It will declutter your fridge and keep your stomach happy.

That's a lot of information to remember so for easy recall, remember this simple rhyme I made just for you.

*Chill cooked food within two hours, or one hour if outside. You'll get five
more days to enjoy, so open wide.
Chuck an egg that floats or gray meat, chicken, and fish. Always trust
your nose and you won't get sick.*

Hey, I tried.

Your Goal: Cutting Stuff
The Risk: Bleeding; Self-Maiming; Mittens Only Forever

THE LESSON: SHARPEN YOUR KNIFE AND TECHNIQUE

Common Mistakes: Ever need to slice a bun, cut fruit, chop vegetables, or open a package? Using the wrong tool, technique, or angle can be a recipe for disaster and sends over 350,000 people to the ER each year. So, pay attention, folks, and you can keep the tip! (Get it? Ha! Ha!)

Recommended Approach: A good sharp knife is awesome. You didn't expect that? A dull knife is your enemy. It requires more force, making it prone to slipping and causing injuries. You're also more apt to be careful with sharp knives. So, invest in a good knife sharpener. Here are some other great tips:

- Putting It Down: Ditch the "hand-held" approach. Place the item you're cutting on a stable cutting board or counter. This prevents wobbling and provides a secure platform for your knife work.
- Slice Away: Remember, direction matters! Always slice away from your body, minimizing the risk of accidental cuts caused by slippage. Frisbee motion not hari-kiri.
- Fingertip Protection: When chopping or dicing on a stable countertop, curl your fingers under the item you're cutting, keeping your fingertips safely away from the blade. A dinged knuckle is better than a sliced fingertip, any day!
- Fork It Up: For extra stability, especially with round or slippery items like lemons, onions, or apples, use a fork to hold them firmly in place while you slice. This keeps those precious fingers even further from harm's way.
- Focus on the Task: Put down the phone, embrace the inner chef, and resist the urge to multitask while wielding your knife. Treat it with respect, and it will treat you well.
- The Cream Cheese Conundrum: Avoid the temptation to lick the cream cheese, icing or chocolate off that butter knife! While tempting, the blade can easily slice your tongue, leaving a nasty surprise.

Safety in the kitchen starts with proper knife skills. Embrace these recommendations, ditch the careless habits, and keep those fingers happy and healthy for years of culinary adventures!

Your Goal: Microwaving Stuff
The Risk: Fire; Skin Burns; Possible DNA Damage?

THE LESSON: MICROWAVES ARE JUST DIFFERENT

Common Mistakes: Tempted to treat your microwave like a lightning-fast oven? Hold on there, chef! While this kitchen gadget is undeniably magical, its superpowers come with a few caveats. Remember, it's not just a speedy oven— it's a powerful radiation machine capable of heating food to scorching temperatures beyond 200 degrees Fahrenheit. Breathe easy, though, because this radiation is non-ionizing, meaning it doesn't have the DNA-altering powers of X-rays. However, it does use high-frequency radio waves to superheat liquids and zips right through paper, glass, and plastic. So, choose your materials wisely, or you might end up with a ruined meal— and possibly a damaged microwave.

Recommended Approach: To harness the magic of your microwave safely, follow these tips:

- Material Matters: Opt for ovenproof glass and ceramic containers— they're reusable and safe. Avoid aluminum foil, metal rims, stainless steel mugs, and those tiny handles on Chinese takeout containers. These act like shields, causing dangerous sparks and preventing your food from heating properly.
- Plastic Dilemma: Plastic containers and Styrofoam work in a pinch, but they have very low melting points. Don't risk melting your container and releasing potentially harmful BPA chemical toxins into your food.
- Liquid Explosions: Be wary of superheating liquids, sauces and hardboiled eggs. They can quickly reach temperatures beyond their boiling point, creating trapped steam that builds pressure and eventually explodes. This is especially dangerous with thick sauces or when breaking the surface tension of water. Bang!
- Slow and Steady Wins the Race: Instead of blasting your food on high power, consider doubling the cooking time and using a lower power setting (50% is a good start). You can also utilize the programmable

reheat function. Trust me, it's still miraculously, amazingly fast!

Embrace these simple tips and unlock the safe and delicious potential of your microwave. With a little knowledge and caution, you can enjoy the magic without the mayhem.

Your Goal: Stovetop Cooking
The Risk: Fire; Burning; Smoke Inhalation

THE LESSON: YOUR COOKING PAN TYPE MATTERS

Common Mistakes: Graduated from grilled cheese to eggs and pancakes, but still battling smoke, burned food, and kitchen chaos? It's likely you haven't mastered the art of understanding your pan. Do you know your pan? Pan, meet Peter. Peter. Pan. Just like people, different pans have unique personalities and require specific approaches to prevent sticking and culinary disasters.

The issue? We often hold onto our beloved pans long after their prime, especially non-stick ones. Once scratched, chipped, or scrubbed with the wrong tools, these once-magical tools become frustrating foes.

Recommended Approach: Let's unlock the secrets of your pan and turn you into a confident kitchen magician.

- Pan Personality Test: Identify your pan's true identity – is it a non-stick socialite, a cast iron warrior, or a stainless steel athlete? Each has its own benefits, quirks and specific directions.
- Oil of Choice: Choose wisely! Opt for oils with high smoking points like ghee (my personal favorite), canola, sunflower, sesame, avocado, or peanut. They'll handle the heat without burning like butter typically does.
- Iron and Steel Buddies: Preheat your pan for a few minutes – think of it as a warm-up session. Then, add your chosen oil or ghee and wait for that shimmer before inviting your food to the party.
- Non-Stick Nemesis: Okay, maybe not a nemesis, but a delicate friend. You should add oil or ghee early and can start cooking it after a short low/medium temperature preheat. Toss it when it starts showing signs of wear and tear. For the love of all things delicious, ditch the metal spatula! It's the sworn enemy of your non-stick surface.
- Pan Pampering: Google your pan's preferred cleaning method. I'm a fan of the simple salt and wet paper towel scrub – it's gentle yet effective. A well-maintained pan is a happy pan!

By understanding your pan and its needs, you can kiss smoke-filled kitchens and burnt offerings goodbye. Embrace the power of your pan, and watch your culinary skills skyrocket!

Your Goal: Making Frozen Pizza
The Risk: Oven Damage; Angering the Pizza Gods; Fire

THE LESSON: HEAVEN IS NEVER FROZEN

Common Mistakes: Ah, pizza. The quintessential comfort food, the life of the party, the ultimate symbol of cheesy goodness. You nailed it once, following the instructions to a T. Now you think all frozen pizzas are created equal. Wouldn't that be a dream? But is it cheese or three-meat supreme? Rising dough or thin crust? Soft or crispy? The cooking process is never the same! Ignoring these differences is why your pizza ended up burnt and stuck to the oven grates, with pepperoni smoldering on the toaster oven coils. Let's face it, pizza is too good to be treated with such disrespect. Time to toss away those bad habits and embrace the secrets to pizza perfection!

Recommended Approach: I confess, frozen pizza isn't my jahn. As a native Philadelphian, my loyalty lies with local pizzerias and the art of the fold. But if frozen is your only option, listen up. You need a pizza stone, the superhero of evenly cooked pizzas. Pre-heat the stone in your oven as it reaches temperature, though be warned: it gets hotter than a jalapeno's armpit! Once the stone is ready, place your pizza on it and watch the magic happen. This culinary companion not only ensures even cooking, but also makes cleanup a breeze. Just wipe it down with a damp paper towel after it cools, and voilà, it's ready for its next mission.

Some frozen pizza's recommend putting them directly on the rack 6-8 inches from the bottom. I suspect that these pizza executives have investments in oven cleaners! Don't let them win. For a few bucks you can own a silicone oven tray liner. Put it on the bottom rack and your pizza on the next highest rack. Any toppings that fall off will be easy to clean up once the oven cools. As for all you toaster oven pizza cooking enthusiasts, I can't help you. I can only pray for you.

Ok, let's get to the real issue here. Just ditch the frozen stuff and find a good Philly- or New York-style pizza shop nearby. Order a large cheese, no fancy crusts or toppings. Thank the owners and staff, then head home and savor the simplicity. Add some hot pepper flakes and a sprinkle of fresh Parmesan, fold it in half, and enjoy. Leftovers? Refrigerate and enjoy a cold slice the next day— Prego!

Your Goal: Food Euphoria
The Risk: Diabetes; Stroke; Pain; Joint Replacement; Death

THE LESSON: DON'T EAT WHAT YOU CAN'T PRONOUNCE

Common Mistakes: We've all been there – lured by the siren song of convenience and long shelf life, devouring ultra-processed, beautifully packaged chemical concoctions that offer fleeting satisfaction but lack real nutritional value. It's a trap, friends, and one that is creating serious health consequences across the globe.

Time to address the elephant in the room. We've been conditioned to shy away from terms like "obese," but let's call it what it is: a medical condition with significant health risks, including pain, heart disease, joint issues, sleep problems, depression, and even a shortened lifespan. A staggering 40% of Americans fall into this category, paying a heavy price in terms of quality of life. It's time to ditch the euphemisms and embrace the truth, because facing it head-on is the first step towards reclaiming our health.

Recommended Approach: Don't let the abundance of diet books overwhelm you. You can do this simply on your terms. Just remember, your quality of life is inextricably linked to your physical health. Here are some simple steps to help you find your food balance:

- Hydrate and Wait: When hunger pangs strike, quench your thirst with a glass of water first. Wait ten minutes – you might be surprised how often thirst masquerades as hunger.
- Shop Smart: Avoid grocery shopping on an empty stomach. Head straight to the outer aisles first where you'll find the bulk of whole foods, nature's fuel for your body. Then you can shop the aisles, but look at the ingredients. If you can't pronounce it, should you eat it?
- Inconvenience is Your Friend: Delete those food delivery apps. If you crave fast food, make a conscious effort of driving to get it. This added inconvenience will likely curb your cravings and prevent mindless ordering.
- Do the Math: Balance your calorie intake with your

activity level. Are you consuming more than you burn? This equation leads to weight gain.

- Unmasking Food Addiction: It's not your fault if you find yourself reaching for unhealthy snacks. Food companies have become experts at manipulating our pleasure centers with potent chemistry. A staggering 60% of our calories come from "ultraprocessed" foods designed to be irresistible. Fight back by making informed choices and prioritizing whole foods.
- Decision Points: Ever kill a bag of Flaming Hot Cheetos or eat a half gallon of ice cream in one sitting? Here's a tip. Add a decision point. Always pour a portion of food into a bowl and put the bag back on the shelf. Researchers have found that when the bowl is empty, you'll most likely NOT fill it again. However, if you just open the bag and start snacking, you'll likely eat more than intended. Try it!

The fight for your health starts on your plate. Ditch the junk, embrace healthy habits, and reclaim your well-being. "Happy Hunger Games! And may the odds be in your favor."

CHAPTER FOUR

LIVE AND LET DRIVE

> *"When I die, I want to go peacefully like my grandfather did, in his sleep, not screaming like the passengers in his car."*

ANONYMOUS

Motor vehicle accidents are number two on the preventable death list! This makes a lot of sense. After all, we do accelerate 4,000-pound plastic and tin boxes toward other – some bigger - plastic boxes, separated only by yellow paint. If you can do that safely, you still must deal with slow idiots, fast maniacs, and distracted a-holes.

Your Goal: Driving Plus Other Stuff
The Risk: Death; Disability; Manslaughter; Jail Time

THE LESSON: MINIMIZE DISTRACTIONS WHILE DRIVING

Common Mistakes: Taking three seconds to find a song, a dropped French fry, or a text seems harmless enough. But at 50 miles per hour, those three seconds translate to driving 75 yards blind! That's a distance you wouldn't cover with your eyes closed on a dare. This is the reality of distracted driving

— a game most people get away with daily. But the question remains: do you feel lucky today? Because, in this case, you're playing probabilities. Eventually, the odds won't be in your favor if you keep playing.

Recommended Approach: Minimize distractions while driving. Let's address the most common culprits: eating, texting, song searching, and daydreaming.

- Create a Buffer of Time and Space: Maintain a three to five-second gap between you and the car ahead. This buffer provides valuable time to react in case of unexpected situations. Watch until the car in front of you passes a line in the road, a mile marker or other object. Keep moving back until it takes five seconds for you to reach that marker.
- Double Your Attention in Busy Areas: Pay extra attention in neighborhoods and city streets. Limited visibility and increased presence of pedestrians, animals, and unpredictable drivers demand heightened awareness.
- Simplify Your Snacks: If you must eat, choose simple options like plain chicken fingers, fries, or burgers. Avoid the fixings, messy sauces, dips, or anything requiring your constant attention. Alternatively, take five minutes to park and enjoy your food. Your safety is worth the brief stop.
- Embrace Hands-Free Technology: Since 2004, Bluetooth has been standard in most cars. Utilize it! Create a playlist before driving and go hands-free. Put your phone on 'Do Not Disturb' and enjoy your music or podcasts.
- Ditch the Texts, Embrace the Call: Received a text? Use your car's hands-free calling feature to chat with the sender. We're not in ancient Egypt anymore; you

don't need hieroglyphics to communicate. Use your voice and enjoy the power of conversation.

The best way to avoid playing the odds of distracted driving is to eliminate distractions altogether. Prioritize your safety and the safety of others by keeping your eyes on the road and your hands on the wheel. Your future self will be so proud of you.

Your Goal: Make up Time
The Risk: Death; Disability; Cost of Tickets and Insurance

THE LESSON: BE EARLY, ALWAYS

Common Mistakes: Many of us are guilty of unrealistic optimism when it comes to estimating travel time. This chronic lateness leads to a cascade of negative consequences: hurried unsafe driving, impatience with others, and general irritation. Imagine a world where everyone arrived early for everything! Wouldn't that be a more pleasant experience for all? You can be the change you wish to see in the world.

Recommended Approach: Adopt this simple mantra: "I am not a late person." On time is no longer an option as being early is your new standard. This shift in mindset unlocks a whole new world of possibilities:

- Need gas? No problem, fill it up.
- Craving coffee? Sure, get some.
- Short on cash? Plenty of time for a quick ATM stop.

You'll have ample time for life's little necessities. This buffer strategy will help eliminate your "need" for fast driving, tailgating, running lights, and other hazardous behaviors.

Here's how to plan it. For every scheduled event, be it work, a doctor's appointment, a haircut, or a dinner reservation—subtract twenty minutes from the start time. This is your new target arrival time.

- Dinner at 7:00? Aim for 6:40.
- Meeting Mom at noon? Arrive by 11:40.
- Work starts at 8:00? Park at 7:40 and get settled.

Your doctor's office understands the need for a buffer, which is why they often request a 15-20 minute early arrival. Listen to them!

By adhering to this strategy, you'll reap the immediate rewards of promptness: reduced stress, positive vibes, and recognition from others for your timeliness. And if you find yourself awkwardly early, don't fret! Utilize the extra time to clean out your inbox, catch up on news, or simply relax and enjoy the peace and quiet. Hey buddy, you've just become the nicest, calmest person ever!

Your Goal: Gotta Go
The Risk: Legal Fees; Fines; Jail Time; Injury; Regret

THE LESSON: DRIVING'S UNNECESSARY

Common Mistakes: We've all overestimated our abilities at some point, especially when tired, under the influence, or simply feeling invincible. The irony? We expect humans in compromised states to make rational decisions, which, unsurprisingly, often leads to poor choices. Prioritizing convenience over safety in these critical moments is a recipe for disaster. Not to mention the terrifying experience of being a passenger with an impaired driver. Let's explore some alternative paths to ensure everyone reaches their destination safely.

Recommended Approach: Anticipation and prevention are your best friends because, as we discussed, your judgment will be clouded when faced with these decisions. Let's tackle tiredness first. Pull over at a safe location, preferably a rest stop. Grab your favorite caffeinated beverage, chug it down, set a timer for 25 minutes, recline your seat, and close your eyes. This "Nappuccino" is a proven way to sharpen your alertness when the caffeine kicks in as you open your eyes.

Secondly, avoid drowsiness-inducing medications before driving or operating heavy machinery. This one's a no-brainer!

Now, let's address the biggest problem: alcohol. It's the leading cause of impaired driving fatalities. Thankfully, we live in an era of readily available rideshare services like Uber, Lyft, and other rideshares and jitneys. Utilize these lifesavers to get you *to* and *from* parties, bars, bonfires, and beyond! Without your car, driving becomes a non-issue. Problem solved! Brilliant, right? For just a few dollars, you can literally buy yourself another day.

Need to be more discreet? Drive to a friend's house and then use a rideshare from there. Split the cost – it's a small price to pay for peace of mind. Worried about your parents' reaction? Well, consider this: lying versus dying? I'm giving you the green light to fib in this scenario. Just make it convincing. And if you get caught, that's on you. But please, just don't get behind the wheel or ride with someone who's impaired. It's not worth the risk.

Your Goal: Reality GTA
The Risk: Injury; Fines; Not So Flattering News Footage

THE LESSON: DRIVE DEFENSIVELY

Common Mistakes: You feel a liberated, powerful and as anonymous as a burner social media account when behind the wheel. You're not. And on a ten-point scale of driving skills, you're most likely a four—at best. Road rage is a criminal offense and has moved up as a top reason for motor vehicle accidents! You can cause road rage, or you can be baited into being angry at others. Let's avoid both. Namaste.

Recommended Approach: Road rage often ignites from aggressive driving. Speeding, tailgating, weaving in and out of traffic, passing on the right, ignoring right-of-way, flashing lights, and honking excessively – these behaviors can turn even the most patient driver into a raging inferno. If you find yourself engaging in any of these, take a deep breath, apologize to anyone you might have offended, and change your ways.

Encountering a road rager? The best defense is a good offense –get out of the way, avoid eye contact, and call 911 immediately. Take note of their car description, mark your location, and report it to the authorities hands-free. You could be a hero and save lives!

Instead of fueling the fire, practice defensive driving. If you want to get someone's attention, use your lights and horn passively. A friendly "toot-toot," is a gentle way to let others know you're there without inciting anger. It's a safe and effective way to share the road without causing unnecessary conflict.

Unfortunately, the road is for everyone, even jerks.

Your Goal: Just Gas 'n Go

The Risk: Accidents; Huge Bills; Flying Off a Cliff, Rolling Seventy-Two Times Down a Mountainside, and Bursting into Flames

THE LESSON: CAR CARE PAYS OFF

Common Mistakes: Let's face it, ignoring those blinking dashboard lights and skipping oil changes isn't exactly a recipe for car longevity. It's like expecting your phone to work perfectly after dropping it in a swimming pool – not gonna

happen. Low fluids, from oil to windshield wiper cleaner, always lead to trouble. And don't even get me started on tires. Good tires are way more important than fancy drivetrain options. And you generally can't spot dangerously low tire pressure unless the car is leaning like a Cholo – which is too late. So, buckle up, because we're about to roll into some car care 101.

Recommended Approach: Here's the secret to avoiding costly repairs and tire-related mishaps— schedule regular maintenance. Schedule oil changes with tire rotations every 7,500 miles/6 months – it's like a spa day for your car. Most service stations will include fluid checks and tire wear inspections as part of the package. This might set you back around $100 twice a year, but trust me, it'll save you thousands in the long run. Pro tip: stick with conventional oil unless your owner's manual specifies otherwise – synthetics can drain your wallet fast.

Do a little DIY. Auto service labor costs alone range from $110 to $200 per hour! So, pay yourself fifty bucks to do the simple things. Changing your engine air filter and cabin air filter is easier than you think. Check your owner's manual for the recommended replacement intervals and grab some new filters from a big box store or online. You got this!

Now, let's talk tires. All-season tires with decent tread are your best friend, and you don't need to break the bank for premium brands. Do your research and consider used tires (always buy two at a time for even wear). Remember, proper inflation is key for tire longevity and fuel efficiency. Don't forget, temperature changes can affect pressure, so check it regularly with the seasons.

And for the love of all things automotive, please pay attention to your dashboard! Those yellow and red lights are there for a reason. Addressing them immediately could lead to a simple, cheap fix. Ignoring them could result in a breakdown in the middle of nowhere… at night… by a cornfield. So, be proactive and address any issues promptly. Remember, a little preventative maintenance goes a long way towards happy, inexpensive car ownership and smooth travels!

CHAPTER FIVE
THRIVE NINE TO FIVE

"While on a ladder, never step back to admire your work."

ANONYMOUS

About 3 million Americans suffer non-fatal injuries and illnesses at work. Obviously, some jobs are riskier than others, but all have hazards. If you find yourself around machinery, in a restaurant, a hospital, a construction site, or a delivery truck, you are high risk! For everyone else, you can also use these tips at work or at home.

Your Goal: Lift and Load
The Risk: Severe Irreversible Back Pain; Misery; Living a Sad Country Song

THE LESSON: WATCH YOUR BACK

Common Mistakes: "Put your back into it!", is a common phrase used to motivate people. Good advice though? According to the Mayo Clinic, back pain often stems from muscle and ligament injuries caused by improper lifting, poor posture, and a lack of exercise. In the US alone, over a million back injuries occur at work every year, accounting for a whopping 20% of all workplace injuries. But guess what? It's entirely preventable!

Chronic back pain is an epidemic, largely due to our delicate back and the intricate network of nerves within. It's a thief that can rob you of your job, relationships, and even dignity. Chronic pain is a humbling experience, to say the least. But you're young and strong, right? Well, that doubled over guy in chronic pain was young and strong once too.

Recommended Approach: Before you tackle anything heavier than two gallons of water, remember the magic word: LEGS. Your legs are your back's best friend!

1. Squat low: Get low with your back straight, channeling your inner sumo wrestler.
2. Hug it tight: Embrace the object for optimal leverage.
3. Leg power: Stand up straight, using the power of your legs to lift the object.
4. Shoulders are off-limits: Keep heavy objects below shoulder height.
5. No twisting: Avoid turning or twisting your body while holding the load.

Imagine yourself as a robot with a rigid, inflexible spine. No bending, no twisting, just pure, efficient lifting. Bonus points for adding some cool robot sound effects!

Your Goal: Get 'er Done
The Risk: Overexertion; Repetitive Task Injuries

THE LESSON: TAKE BREAKS

Common Mistakes: We've all been there: lost in the workday vortex, skipping breaks and meals in an attempt to conquer our to-do lists. But for you desk jockeys, this can lead to a literal pain in the neck i.e. tech neck. And for our labor-intensive friends, being stuck in the same position can pinch nerves faster than you can say "ouch!" Working nonstop also dehydrates us and zaps our concentration, making us more susceptible to mistakes. Remote workers – pay attention!

Recommended Approach: While specific break rules are determined by employers (especially for "clock punchers"), this isn't about micromanaging your schedule. It's about a simple mantra: Ten-four, good buddy. Every four hours take ten minutes to do something different. First and foremost, hydrate! Grab some water, tea, or your beverage of choice to replenish your body. Then, take ten minutes away from your job.

Desk warriors, stop typing and give your hands and wrists some TLC with massages and rotations. Stand up, do some squats or walk in place, and stretch your fingers skyward while taking deep breaths. Your body will thank you.

And our fellow laborers, kitchen wizards, and service providers who spend their days on their feet? Consider a midday sock change – you'd be surprised how refreshing it is! Remember to keep your core engaged and your back straight – good posture fights fatigue like a champ.

So, take those breaks, move your body, and recharge your batteries. It's not just good for your health, it's good for your productivity and your sanity.

Your Goal: Take Shortcuts
The Risk: Mangled Limbs; Horrible YouTube Footage

THE LESSON: IT'S FINE...UNTIL IT ISN'T

Common Mistakes: We all think we can get away with it. "It'll be fine," we say, as we skip safety glasses, bypass equipment shields, or ignore the call for hearing protection. But those, my friends, are the infamous "last words" we hear in countless workplace accident reports. This isn't just about following the rules; it's about protecting yourself, your colleagues, and your loved ones. There are approximately 8,000 avoidable work injuries every day in the United States! So, no matter your dominant hand, you have to do this "righty".

Recommended Approach: This isn't about rules, it's about mindset. If you undergo safety training, wear protective gear, or operate machinery (not to mention fryers, ovens, and their fiery brethren), then this mantra is for you: Never compromise safety, for yourself or your coworkers. Nine out of ten workplace injuries are caused by unsafe acts, often stemming from carelessness, distraction, or complacency. That means if something happens, it's not just an accident – it's a consequence of your choices i.e. it's your fault. Choose to live free from pain and guilt.

Talk to your coworkers about their experiences. You'll be treated to a wild array of stories! Consider that a lot of safety rules stem from previous horrific accidents. John might share his close call with losing an eye, or Sandy might detail her triple-femur fracture adventure. Sadly, you might also hear about someone who didn't live to tell. It all comes down to mindset. Choose life, and choose to tell different stories.

So, ditch the shortcuts, embrace a safety-first mindset, and live to tell another tale. It's not just about the rules; it's about creating a safe and healthy environment for everyone.

CHAPTER SIX

PARTY ABYSMAL

"Last night I let the party get the best of me."

WIZ KHALIFA

It's the end of the week, and it's party time! Go on, you've earned it. Consider though, that Netflix could probably create a whole category of movies about terrible things that happen at parties. Oh, and remember that "funny" is stuff that happens to other people. Regardless of your alcohol or recreational drug use intentions, consider these tips for a safe and fun night out or in.

Your Goal: Quick Buzz
The Risk: Sexual Assault; Falls; Overdose; Car Accidents

THE LESSON: STAY ALERT AND COHERENT

Common Mistakes: Ever thought of skipping a meal and pre-gaming with rum and Coke? You'll likely end up over-spending and/or overindulging anyway, leading to a night of regret, not revelry. Ladies, those "free" clubs with bottomless drinks? There's a reason they're free – and it's not because the club is overflowing with generosity. You're bait. And that charming stranger who offers you a drink? While their intentions might be good, remember, any unattended beverage is an invitation for trouble. These are just a few common scenarios that can turn your night into a horror story instead of a comedy.

Recommended Approach: Here's a radical idea: consider a sober life. I know, I know, it's crazy. But seriously, think about it. Ok, for the rest of you, the key is to know your limits. Before heading out, eat a proper meal at home. This will help slow down alcohol absorption and prevent you from making impulsive decisions. Then, set a budget for the night and withdraw that amount in cash. Once the cash is gone, it's a natural stopping point, giving you a chance to re-evaluate and stick to your plan. (No tapping!)

Another tip: alternate your alcoholic drinks with water. This will help you stay hydrated and pace yourself. Avoid caffeinated and energy drinks, as they mask the effects of alcohol, leading to overconsumption. And be aware of carbonated alcoholic beverages, as they speed up alcohol absorption. The key is to feel the impairment gradually so you can adjust vs. having it hit you like a brick - lights out!

Finally, be wary of those charming strangers offering drinks and only accept drinks directly from the bartender. Never leave your drink unattended, and if you need to step away, ditch it and order a fresh one.

The key is to find your happy place and hold. If you can manage that, you'll not only save money but also protect your health, dignity, and safety. So, ditch the regret and embrace responsible drinking. Enjoy yourself, but do it smartly.

Your Goal: Make an Impression
The Risk: Paralysis; Concussion; Embarrassment

THE LESSON: BE POSITIVELY MEMORABLE

Common Mistakes: So, you pulled a stunt at a party once, got a laugh (or maybe a cringe), and somehow managed to escape unscathed. Now you think this is your ticket to popularity? Pump the brakes. The funny thing is, you might not even know if they were laughing *at* you or *with* you. Typically, the "funny" stuff involves water, fire, a pickup truck, or some unholy combination of all three. Oh, and let's not forget gravity – that loves to make a grand entrance when alcohol is involved.

The truth is you can be memorable without becoming the party idiot who ends up in an ambulance. Let's explore some alternative routes to social success!

Recommended Approach: Getting noticed is actually easier than you think. No need to learn magic tricks (unless you can pull something off with a cup, a toothpick or a few straws— please no fake flower or bunnies). The real magic lies in the art of conversation. Consider Dale Carnegie's *How to Win Friends and Influence People.* How about Googling "funny conversation starters"? Something like, "Do you know any funny conversation starters?" or "So, when was the last time you faked being sick?" works wonders to get things going. Bonus points if you can befriend the host – they're your ticket to social circles.

Taking a page from Napoleon Dynamite and learning some sweet moves never hurts. Everyone loves a good dancer! And speaking of music, consider becoming the party's music guru. Read the vibe, and if the moment is right, take control of the tunes with your killer playlist or freestyle your way into hearts. Remember, you're tight with the host now, right?

Finally, never underestimate the power of a good outfit. When you look good, you feel good, and that confidence shines brighter than any spotlight. So, relax, have fun, and leave the ambulance rides to the other guy. The key to social success is to be clever, not reckless. Be the person people remember for the right reasons, not the one they laugh at (or shake their heads at) later. Now go out there and rock that party!

Your Goal: Ignore the Signs
The Risk: Poisoning; Cirrhosis of the Liver; Death

THE LESSON: HELP YOUR FRIENDS

Common Mistakes: Let's say you have a friend who got a DUI, skips class, pulls all-nighters to catch up on missed work, and sports a GPA that looks like it tumbled down a flight of stairs. Or maybe they black out frequently, or boast about their "high tolerance" – basically, drinking everyone under the table until the money runs out, the party ends, or the bar closes. Did you know that the age group most likely to struggle with alcohol use disorder is between 18 and 30? If you have a friend exhibiting these red flags, it's time to step up and offer your support.

Recommended Approach: There's no guaranteed one-size-fits-all solution, but there are plenty of things you can do to help. Approach your friend with these key points:

- Timing is everything: Don't try to have this conversation when they're under the influence. Wait until they're sober and clear-headed.
- Keep it calm: Avoid confrontation and accusatory language. Instead, focus on expressing your concern and offering support.
- Use "I" statements: This helps your friend focus on your feelings and perspective, rather than feeling attacked or blamed. Examples include: "I really care about you" or "I've noticed you've been acting differently lately." You can also express specific observations, like "I've missed you in class and it seems like you've been going out a lot" or "I'm just wondering if everything is okay."

Having other friends involved can also be incredibly helpful. Remember, this is a journey, not a destination. By planting that seed of concern and offering your support, you could be making a life-altering difference for your friend. Studies show that even one individual counseling session can significantly reduce a lifetime of substance misuse and abuse. So, if the initial conversation goes well, encourage them to seek professional help. You could be saving their life.

CHAPTER SEVEN
CALL OF THE WILD

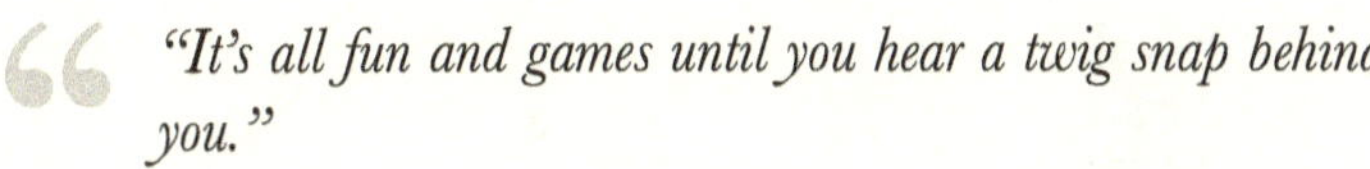

"It's all fun and games until you hear a twig snap behind you."

ANONYMOUS

You made it to the weekend, and it's time for some outdoor activities! You know that dog of yours in the sweater with a bow in her hair that will only eat wild caught salmon? Yeah, that was a wolf once. Sorry to say, you're the same. Our ancestors would be shocked at how vulnerable we are outdoors. It's not reversible without a lot of training so let's try to keep you safe out there in the wild!

Your Goal: Brown Up
The Risk: Heat Stroke; Sunburn; Skin Cancer

THE LESSON: SUN WORSHIP RESPONSIBLY

Common Mistakes: We often underestimate the sun's power, dismissing it as a distant star that gifts us with light and warmth. But the truth is, the sun's ultraviolet (UV) radiation packs a punch, causing premature aging, skin cancer, and even eye damage like cornea burns. Sure, these are mostly "future-self" problems, but UV exposure also creates 'today' problems like a weakened immune system. This means you're likely to get sick more often including being more susceptible to nasty cold sores and herpes outbreaks Are you paying attention yet?

Recommended Approach: Let's face it, we all grab an umbrella when it's raining and probably should do the same for sunshine. Think of UV rays like invisible dangerous raindrops falling from the sky especially between 10:00 a.m. and 4:00 p.m. Don't be fooled by clouds or clothing, either as UV rays penetrate right through! These rays bounce off sand, water, snow, and pavement, ensuring you're never truly safe from their reach.

Here's your sun-safety cheat sheet:

- 15/15: Apply sunscreen with SPF 15 or higher at least 15 minutes before sun exposure and reapply every two hours.
- Hattitude: Hats are your best friends on sunny days. A good bucket hat can protect your sensitive scalp if you have short or thinning hair. And the rim of most hats may save your nose from blistering.
- Shades that shade: Don't settle for sunglasses that just look cool – choose ones that block UV rays.
- Hydrate or die-drate: Drink plenty of water or electrolyte beverages throughout your day, especially when outdoors. Clear urine is a sign of proper hydration so if you're not peeing at all or your pee is dark yellow, you're at risk. Also, keep an eye out for symptoms like pale or clammy skin, headache, and dizziness. These are early signs of heatstroke, which can be fatal if not addressed promptly within an hour.

Stay cool, stay hydrated, and stay safe under the sun. Your healthy glow and smooth skin will thank you!

Your Goal: Trailblaze
The Risk: Falls; Chronic Infectious Diseases; Poisoning

THE LESSON: PREP FOR EVERY HIKE

Common Mistakes: So, you've got a hike planned—awesome! I'm a big fan of spending time outdoors! But, before you throw on your gym shorts, Crocs, and that vintage concert tee, let's have a quick reality check. Unless you're strolling on a paved path, your outfit choice just skyrocketed your risk for trouble!Did you know nearly 500,000 Americans get Lyme disease each year from tiny, blacklegged ticks, a disease that can become chronic if not treated quickly? And vibrant poison ivy, oak, and sumac plants are thriving. They're responsible for about 40,000 ER visits annually. Oh, and you might be one of the four in 1,000 with a severe bee allergy, so we must avoid stings. And then there's falls and slips which are the most common hiking injuries, leading to over 15,000 search and rescue operations in the US each year. Yikes!

Recommended Approach: I want you to have a great time exploring in nature because it is one of the healthiest things humans can do! I even wrote another book about it called *Calm Outside*. Here's your guide to a safe and enjoyable trek:

- Stick to the Trail: Stay on the marked path to avoid getting lost or encountering hidden dangers.
- Watch the Time: Plan your hike with daylight in mind, and stick to your schedule to avoid getting caught out after dark.
- Gear Up: Ditch the flimsy footwear and opt for sturdy hiking boots or shoes with good ankle support and a good grip. Long-sleeved shirts, long socks and pants protect you from insects and plants. Pick a fabric that's appropriate for the weather, and stick to light colors.
- Beware of Poisonous Plants: Remember the saying, "Leaves of three, let them be!" Steer clear of any plant with three leaves growing together, like poison ivy, oak, and sumac. And for the love of all things good, please don't use those plants for toilet paper! (I may be speaking from experience.)
- Avoid Stinging Insects: Skip the sweet-smelling lotions and deodorants, as they act like bee and wasp magnets. If a stinger starts buzzing your way, stay

calm and slowly back away. Swatting only makes
them angry!
- Tick Check: When hiking in wooded areas, ticks are
  inevitable. To protect yourself from Lyme disease, I'll
  repeat that you should wear light-colored long-
  sleeved shirts, long socks, and pants. After your hike,
  wipe down exposed skin with a wet wipe and
  meticulously check for ticks. They like to travel, so do
  a second check in the shower later.
- Step with Care: Watch your feet! Step *over* rocks,
  fallen trees, large roots, and anything else that could
  fall apart and cause a slip or twisted ankle. Avoiding a
  fall is easier than recovering from one.

Now, go forth and conquer those trails! But most importantly,
hike smart and have fun!

Your Goal: Mow or Less
The Risk: Amputation; Blindness; Infection

THE LESSON: PRACTICE YARD SMARTS

Common Mistakes: Ah, yard work. The perfect opportunity to bask in the sun land get a tan while tackling those overgrown weeds, right? Ah…nope. Combining tanning with yard work often results in outfit choices like shorts, flip-flops, or even worse, bare feet. Improper clothing, impatience, frustration, fatigue, and blades spinning at supersonic speeds – it's a recipe for disaster! Yard work leads to over 100,000 emergency room visits each year due to mower mishaps and other power tool injuries. But fear not, fellow gardener, there's a way to keep your lawn green without accidentally splattering it red.

Recommended Approach: Let's talk safety gear before you tackle that unruly lawn. Your main enemies are flying projectiles like sticks, pebbles, bugs, and the occasional stray toe or finger. So, gear up properly:

- Eye protection: While there are lots of sunglasses designs, you can only count on wrap arounds. Or better yet, opt for tinted safety glasses or goggles to keep your eyes safe from debris.
- Leg and foot protection: Jeans and closed-toe shoes are your best friends here. Protect those precious toes! They can be hard to find if they are lopped off.
- Hand protection: Any work gloves help, but cowhide gloves are your best weapon against cuts, scrapes, and infections.

Let's talk tools! Power tools are amazing, but they come with built-in safety features for a reason. Don't be tempted to "hack" them— trust me, those features are there because someone learned the hard way.

- Beware the tangled web: When a string or vine gets caught in the blades or wires, stay calm and turn off the machine immediately.
- Gas-powered guzzlers: Be mindful of spills and flooding when refueling or operating gas-powered tools.

- Battery-powered buddies: Always remove the battery before fiddling with your tools.

A little preparation and awareness can go a long way towards keeping you safe and sound while you conquer your yard. Now go forth and cultivate your green haven.

Your Goal: Heat and Sizzle
The Risk: Bursting into Flames; Making Smokey the Bear Cry; Gasping for Air

THE LESSON: PRACTICE FLAME SAFETY

Common Mistakes: Ah, the allure of a crackling fire pit and the joys of outdoor cooking! But hold on, fire dragons. According to the American Lung Association, while fire is mesmerizing, it's not without health concerns. I love good fires, so here are ways to minimize smoke and fire hazards while still enjoying our s'mores. Let's also address those 20,000 annual visits to the ER and the 5,000 house fires caused by grill masters.

Recommended Approach: Before you burn, learn! Firstly, remember that smoke is a nuisance for neighbors and a nightmare for people with respiratory sensitivities. Ensure individuals with lung conditions are positioned away from the smoke and have easy access to masks and inhalers.

Next, minimize smoke by choosing dry, seasoned firewood and ensuring proper ventilation. Dry wood is typically darker, has cracks in the end grain, and produces a hollow sound when struck against another piece. Avoid burning anything except wood, including leaves. Keep the fire burning hot to avoid smoldering, which produces more smoke. And finally, take Smokey Bear's advice to heart: "Only you can prevent forest fires." Completely extinguish the fire with dirt, rocks, or yes, even pee.

Now, let's talk grilling safety! Most issues arise from gas grill leaks. To check for leaks, turn on the grill and apply soapy water to the entire hose. Bubbles indicate a dangerous leak so immediately shut everything off and replace the hose. Keep your grill clean and empty the drip pan regularly— grease buildup is a major fire hazard. If a grease fire occurs, close the lid and slowly turn off the gas. Fire extinguishers can spread grease fires, so resist the urge to use them.

And lastly, don't forget your furry friend! Leash your dog around small footprint grills like charcoal grills. The enticing aroma of food can turn them into excited lunatics, leading to accidental grill knockdowns.

By following these tips, you can enjoy the magic of fire and grilling without compromising safety. Remember, knowledge is power, and a little preparation goes a long way in ensuring a safe and enjoyable outdoor experience.

CHAPTER EIGHT
OCEAN'S EXCEPTION

"If you need to reach me, call me on my shell."

ANONYMOUS

More of a beach-or-pool weekender? I get it. Just remember—drowning ranks as the fifth-leading cause of accidental death. So yeah, we're going to dive into that. Water can be both simple and sneaky: it's either helping you float or trying to pull you under. This chapter's about how to enjoy it safely—and how to know when to get the heck out of the water before it turns on you.

Your Goal: Fresh Water Fun
The Risk: Drowning; Paralysis; Brain Damage

THE LESSON: BE A SMART SWIMMER

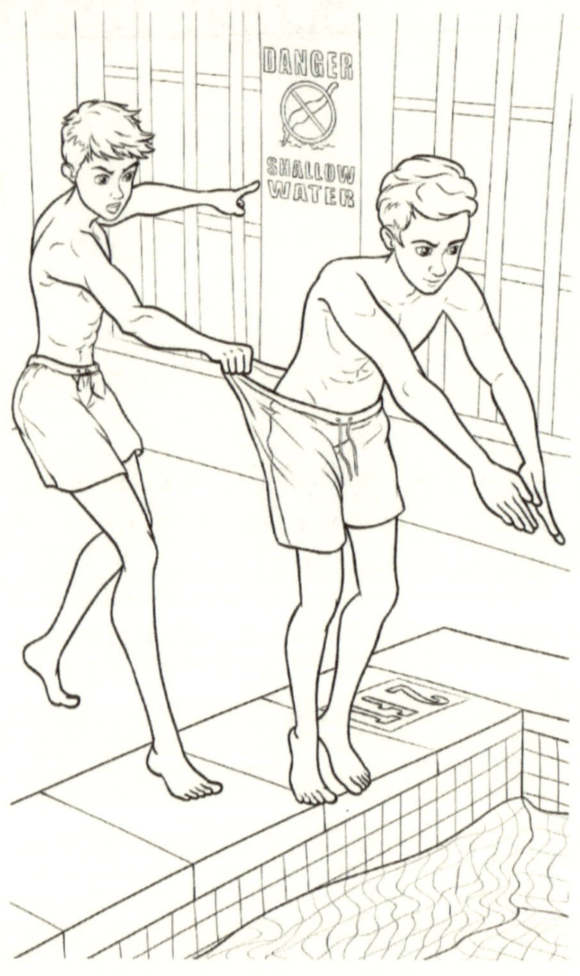

Common Mistakes: You learned to swim as a kid, maybe even dominated the middle school swim team. What could possibly go wrong? Well friend, lakes, oceans, quarries, and rivers are far from your backyard pool or the gym's controlled environment. Water depth, temperature, density, currents, waves, boats, and even aquatic life come into play, making these natural bodies of water a whole different ball game. In fact, about 90% of all drownings occur in freshwater like rivers and lakes, compared to a relatively small number in swimming pools. Let's dive in and explore how to stay safe in the water!

Recommended Approach: Some say we evolved from creatures of the sea, but there's not much evidence of that today! Follow these tips to stay safe in fresh water:

- Practice makes perfect: Before you hit the open water, brush up on your swimming, floating, and paddling skills. This is the single most important thing you can do to prevent drowning.
- Alcohol is not a water buddy: Alcohol is involved in a staggering 50% of fatal drownings. So, keep your drinking to a minimum or better yet, skip it altogether when you're swimming.
- Safety in numbers: Drownings often occur when people are alone or go unnoticed. Always swim with friends or family and implement the buddy system to ensure everyone's safety.
- Respect the water: Rivers and lakes harbor hidden dangers like deceptive currents, sudden drop-offs, and unpredictable cold spots. Even water as warm as 70 degrees Fahrenheit (21 degrees Celsius), can produce spasms causing you to hyperventilate and swallow or aspirate water.
- Embrace the life preserver: This isn't just a great name for a product – it's a life-saving tool. Put it on your birthday wish list so you can get one that fits well, looks cool, and increases your chances of wearing it.

- **Feet first, always**: Avoid diving headfirst into unknown waters. It's estimated that about 1,000 people suffer a spinal cord injury from diving each year! Always jump in feet first, especially the first time, to ensure the depth is safe and there are no hidden obstructions that could cause injuries.

Following these tips can help you enjoy your time in the water without becoming a statistic.

Your Goal: Have a Beach Day
The Risk: Paralysis; Drowning; Twisted Limbs; Flesh- and Brain-Eating Amoebas

THE LESSON: WATCH THE SIGNS AT THE SHORE

Common Mistakes: So, you've embarked on your dream vacation, only to encounter beach closures, bad weather, or overwhelming crowds. Feeling frustrated? Don't let it cloud your judgment! Suck it up, buttercup, and avoid making matters worse with risky behavior that could leave you with a jellyfish sting, bacterial infection, or – although less likely – a lightning strike.

Recommended Approach: First and foremost, pay attention to the signs. Any flag fluttering on the beach should raise a… red flag… in your mind. Here's a quick rundown:

- Single red flag: Do *not* go in the water.
- Double red flag: Strong currents are lurking – stay dry!
- Purple flag: Dangerous marine life is present – think twice before hitting the waves. (Seriously, so I really have to convince you to obey purple?)

Did you know that rip currents cause over 80% of ocean rescues? If you find yourself swept away by one, don't panic and try to fight it head-on. Instead, swim parallel to the shore and then back to land at an angle.

Next, watch out for 'Shorebreaks', where waves abruptly transition from deep to shallow water and crash hard. These can be real spine-busters, so proceed carefully!

Playing in the ocean comes with the inevitable: seawater ingestion. Be prepared for a salty splash in your sinuses and stomach. You may need a little Pepto later.

Red tides and water quality warnings are serious. Stay out of the water if these are present, unless you like ER visits. Also, avoid swimming near areas where water flows from land into the sea, as these are often contaminated with fertilizers, chemicals, and sewage. Gross!

Finally, be wary of warm water. Temperatures above 80 degrees Fahrenheit significantly increase the risk of bacterial infections. Not the souvenir you were hoping for!

By following these simple tips, you can turn your beach vacation into a fun and safe experience. The ocean is a powerful force – respect it, and it will respect you back. Now go forth and enjoy the sun, sand, and surf... safely!

Your Goal: Have a Deep Sea Day
The Risk: Painful Wounds; Vomiting; Limb Loss

THE LESSON: PREP FOR OCEAN ADVENTURES

Common Mistakes: Someone suggests a deep-sea fishing trip and you're instantly on board! But hold on a second. Did you know that no one is truly immune to sea sickness? It's a natural brain thing. And nearly 30% of people experience it severely which can be brutal. And guess what? Fishing and snorkeling contribute to a whopping 100,000 accidents each year. Let's make sure your ocean adventure is filled with fun memories and picture-perfect moments, not nausea and mishaps!

Recommended Approach: Feeling nervous about seasickness? Fear not, land lubber! Here are some tricks to keep your stomach happy:

- Pre-game like a pro: The day before your trip, steer clear of coffee, alcohol, and spicy food. Instead, pack ginger chews, mint candies, or lavender essential oils – these are your new anti-nausea best friends. You can also consider taking over-the-counter medication like Antivert or Dramamine.
- Eyes on the horizon: Avoid going below deck, reading, or staring at your phone. Instead, try lying down and closing your eyes.
- Embrace the fresh air: While the boat is moving, find a spot on the deck facing forward, preferably away from the diesel fumes (they make most people sick), and wear your life jacket at all times.

Once the boat anchors for fishing or snorkeling, the worst is over! It's time to dive into the fun.

You made it to your destination! If you got sick it should start to get better. Listen to the captain and follow their instructions closely. If you plan to jump in the water, remember these safety tips:

- Ditch the jewels and bait: Shiny objects like jewelry and dead fish attract predators. Leave them both on the boat!
- Safety in numbers: Always stick with your group and

don't get too far from the boat unless you have a guide.

- Jellyfish, Sea Urchins and Lionfish watch: If the captain warns of jellyfish ask him to pick a different spot. Sea urchins are those spiky balls you want to avoid touching – trust me, it hurts! Caribbean and Western Atlantic snorkelers will likely encounter Lionfish. Lionfish are stunning creatures that pack a venomous punch, so admire them from a safe distance.
- Stingray etiquette: Stingrays aren't aggressive, but don't follow one – you don't want to be on the wrong end of that tail!
- Shark encounter: If you see a shark, stay calm and avoid acting like prey. Don't splash around or swim frantically away, especially if the boat is far. Maintain eye contact and face the shark – this often deters them. If it gets too close, push its nose down and away. Now, if this happens you'll probably poop a little. It's ok, you're alive!

By following these simple tips, you can conquer your fears, enjoy the breathtaking beauty of the ocean, and return home with amazing stories and unforgettable memories. Play it smart, and the ocean will reward you with the experience of a lifetime.

CHAPTER NINE

WORKING THE CROWD

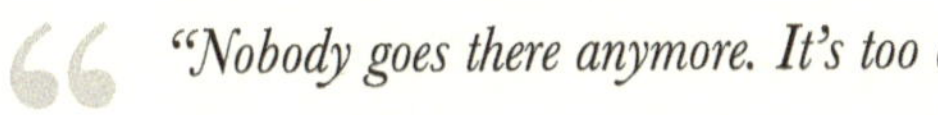

> *"Nobody goes there anymore. It's too crowded."*
>
> YOGI BERRA

You may be in harm's way in a few situations that involve crowds. For instance, you may be travelling to popular cities, going to concerts, or attending large sporting events. Perhaps you encounter a strange person or hear gunfire nearby. As for large crowds of zombies, you already know to destroy the head, right? So these are tips for the situations when everyone is living and not trying to eat you.

Your Goal: Attend the Big Show
The Risk: Getting Crushed or Trampled

THE LESSON: SAFELY NAVIGATE A CROWDED HOUSE

Common Mistakes: Underestimating the power of a crowd is a recipe for trouble. As American philosopher Josiah Royce aptly put it, "A crowd, whether it be a dangerous mob or an amiably joyous gathering at a picnic, is not a community. It has a mind, but no institutions, no organizations, no coherent unity, no history, no traditions." In other words, crowds are unpredictable, and what starts as a fun event can quickly turn deadly. Take the 2022 South Korean Street party, where over 150 people died in a crush. That's a sobering reminder that excitement can morph into tragedy in the blink of an eye. You paid a ridiculous price for those Swiftie tickets so let's go! "Devils roll the dice. Angels roll their eyes." We'll roll safely to the exit!

Recommended Approach: Our goal is to minimize your risk of getting trampled, falling, or losing your cool. Here's how:

- Plan your escape: When you arrive, take a moment to survey the scene and plot your escape routes. Just like an airline attendant reminds everyone, locate the nearest exits and entrances. Think ahead!
- Stay upright: Don't become a casualty of circumstances because you dropped your phone or handbag. Ditch the high heels, flip-flops, and strapless sandals and opt for shoes that offer proper support. If things get dicey and you're stuck in flimsy footwear— go barefoot.
- Create your own space: If the crowd feels suffocating, bend your arms and lift them in front of you like a boxer. Interlace your fingers to create a chest-protecting cage. This simple maneuver can save your life, as many crowd-related deaths occur due to chest compression that restricts breathing.
- Be prepared for the stampede: Even if you're safely ensconced in the nosebleed section, be aware that the exit will likely resemble a cattle drive. Brace yourself for some jostling and close contact.

Remember, safety is paramount. By following these tips and staying alert, you can navigate crowded events with confidence and ensure that your experience is fun and memorable!

Your Goal: Dodge the Bullet
The Risk: Getting Shot, yeah, that's it.

THE LESSON: HOW TO DODGE THE BULLET

Common Mistakes: The framers of the US Constitution's Second Amendment could never have predicted the explosion in population, advancements in firearm technology, and the growing prevalence of mental health issues in today's society.

It's a sobering reality that gun violence claims roughly as many lives in the US each year as car accidents, with a staggering 60-70% of those deaths being suicides. Sadly, the majority of remaining gun fatalities involve young males between the ages of 15 and 29. Unfortunately, music festivals, political rallies, parades, movie theaters, schools and malls have been targets for mass murderers. While mass shootings are thankfully rare, affecting about 700 people annually, it's crucial to be prepared for any situation.

Recommended Approach: If you are struggling with suicidal thoughts: You are not alone. Please reach out for help. Dial 988 to connect with a trained crisis counselor who can provide support and resources. Your life is precious, and we need you here.

Understanding and preventing murder is a complex issue that defies simple solutions. However, reflecting on your social circle and activities can provide valuable insights. Trust your gut and avoid situations, friends and gatherings that feel unsafe.

Active shooter situations are often chaotic and fast-paced, but they typically unfold within minutes. Remember, you have the power to survive! Experts recommend three courses of action:

- Run: If escape is possible, run away without hesitation, regardless of whether others follow. Do *not* attempt to move injured individuals.
- Hide: If running isn't an option, find a place to conceal yourself. This should be out of sight and offer protection from gunfire, such as a locked room. Barricade the door with furniture for added security. Silence your phone and any other sources of noise that could attract attention.

- Fight: Only consider engaging the shooter as a last resort. Throw objects and improvise weapons to disrupt and incapacitate them.

When law enforcement arrives:

- Immediately put down any items you're holding.
- Keep your hands visible and raise your arms. Remember, officers see everyone as a potential threat during such situations.
- Remain calm and take deep breaths. You are a survivor!

By understanding the potential risks and adopting these safety strategies, you can navigate the world with greater awareness and confidence.

Your Goal: Trust the Locals
The Risk: Theft; Money Loss; Taking a Severe Beating

THE LESSON: THIEVES ARE SMARTER THAN YOU

Common Mistakes: Ah, the allure of a new city! You're a savvy traveler, right? Street-smart and immune to the wiles of the unscrupulous? Think again! Your brain is hardwired for trust and empathy, making you a prime target for con artists.

Don't worry, it's not your fault – it's human nature. Every con artist knows this, so pay attention. Oh, unless you've *never* been fooled by a magician. Uh huh. Abracadabra!

Recommended Approach: Here's your secret weapon— a healthy dose of skepticism. Treat every local encounter with a cautious eye. Think "better safe than sorry" and don't be afraid to appear rude. Remember, politeness can be a scammer's playground. You can always apologize later, but recovering from a loss or assault is a whole different story.

Rule of thumb: avoid dark alleys and shady characters. Stick to well-lit areas and steer clear of anyone who seems overly friendly or pushy. If someone tries to touch you or slip jewelry onto your wrist, politely decline and walk away. The "lost jewelry" trick is a classic scam to lure you into a purchase or create a scene. "I found this ring by you. Is it yours? It looks expensive. I'll sell it to you for $100." Nope.

Street performers and charity workers are not always what they seem. Be mindful of hidden accomplices in the crowd waiting for the perfect moment to strike while you're distracted.

Pickpockets are also masters of distraction. Invest in an anti-theft cross-body bag and avoid carrying valuables in your back pocket. Pack light for day trips and leave unnecessary items at your accommodation.

Smart planning can save you from a travel nightmare. Store digital copies of your passport, credit cards, and essential documents in a secure cloud or password-protected folder. Diversify your financial safety net by carrying different credit cards with different account numbers than your travel partner. This ensures you can still access funds if one card gets stolen and you have to cancel it.

Follow these tips and you'll be ready to conquer Paris, Washington D.C., or even Tatooine, scam-free and ready for adventure! A little healthy skepticism can go a long way in keeping your travels safe and enjoyable.

Your Goal: Look the Other Way
The Risk: Being Stabbed; Broken Jaw; Guilt

THE LESSON: KNOW WHEN TO DEESCALATE OR DASH

Common Mistakes: It's easy to dismiss someone's erratic behavior as "their problem," especially if they seem rude, angry, or aggressive. However, this can quickly turn into a safety hazard for you and others. While only a small percentage of individuals with serious mental illness resort to violence, it's crucial to know when to de-escalate and when to dash.

Recommended Approach: Witnessing an erratic individual can be unsettling and confusing. If you see someone screaming, clenching fists, throwing objects, or approaching you aggressively— prioritize your safety. Exit the situation as quickly as possible, call 911, and inform the dispatcher that it's a mental health emergency. If escape is not an option, de-escalation becomes your next step.

Remember, shouting "Calm down!" has never calmed anyone down. Trust me, I checked. Instead, maintain your own calmness, speak softly, and be respectful. Focus on compassionate statements like, "I'm sorry you're going through this," "I want to help," and "Help me understand what's upsetting you." Active listening, acknowledging their feelings, and allowing them to express their emotions are key to de-escalation.

Increase your escape opportunities by suggesting alternatives, such as, "Would you like to step outside for some fresh air while we talk?" or "Would you like me to get you a taxi at the next stop?" Remember, you're buying time while help is on its way (you've already called 988 or 911) and maintaining a safe distance. Many people today feel neglected and isolated. Avoid fueling the fire by showing empathy and understanding, and you'll navigate this situation safely.

CHAPTER TEN
CATEGORICALLY WRONG

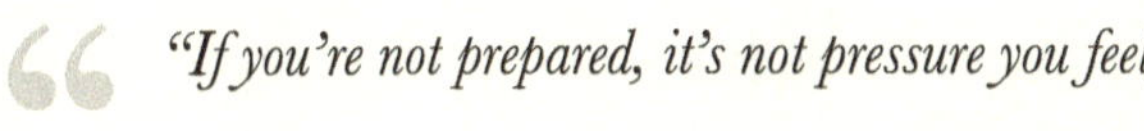

"If you're not prepared, it's not pressure you feel, it's fear."

BRUCE BOCHY

You may be in harm's way in a few other situations that don't fit neatly into one of the other categories but are serious and preventable. We're going to talk about things like dogs, dating and exercising to round out your lessons. You're going to survive your twenty's and it's relatively smooth sailing after that. Start thinking about setting up that retirement account because you'll need money when you're a vibrant, healthy octogenarian.

Your Goal: Dry Your Clothes
The Risk: Burning your clothes and everything around them!

THE LESSON: CLEAN THE DRYER VENT

Common Mistakes: Didn't have to do your own laundry at home? Like many of the situations in this book, we parents just go about our lives hoping you'll figure out how everything works. Which means— you have to figure out how everything works! Case in point: the clothes dryer. On top or inside the door of the dryer is a lint trap. Why? Because the friction, heat, and tumbling of clothes loosen tiny fibers, causing some of them to break free. These little runaway fibers are highly flammable. The lint trap grabs them before they can build up in the vent that snakes outside. Without that catch-net, you'd eventually have a fire in the vent.

But the trap only works if it's clean! A clogged lint screen sends even more fibers down the vent, creating a serious fire hazard inside the dryer itself. According to the U.S. Fire Administration, clothes dryers cause nearly 3,000 home fires every year. And if you have a gas dryer, a blocked vent can lead to carbon monoxide leaking into your home. Beware if your laundry room is a small space—your sleepiness could turn into a permanent dirt nap.

Recommended Approach: The theme of this book has been prevention and preparedness. That means reading product manuals and doing basic maintenance. Here's the simple, safe truth about electric and gas dryers: they generate *a lot* of heat. Even though dryers are regulated not to exceed about 165°F (74°C), metal components, tight spaces, and clogged lint traps can push temperatures past 300°F (150°C)!

To prevent that, make it a habit to pull and clean your lint trap after every load. It's oddly satisfying to gather up that soft, fluffy stuff into a ball. The next step is a little more involved but only needs to be done once a year — and it's fun, too. Move the dryer away from the wall so you can reach the vent hose. Disconnect it and, using a **Shop-Vac** or **leaf blower**, blast that duct clean! You'll probably see a storm of lint balls flying across the yard. Mission accomplished. That was very adult of you!

Your Goal: Pet the Doggy

The Risk: Deep Wounds; Infection; Emotional Trauma

THE LESSON: ALL DOGS CAN BITE

Common Mistakes: Ah, poodle-ee-poo! Who can resist the urge to rush over and shower dogs with affection? But hold on a second. Did you know that over 1,000 people visit the ER **every day** due to dog bites? It's estimated that 4.5 million people are bitten by dogs annually, and about

800,000 of those bites require medical attention. Ouch! According to the American Kennel Club, we often forget that our furry friends aren't human, and this can lead to trouble. You may have noticed that most dogs possess the emotional range of a two-and-a-half-year-old, including joy, love, shyness, fear, and yes, other dreaded "terrible twos" behaviors. And just like those human toddlers, dogs can be unpredictable and prone to sudden outbursts. Unless you're comfortable facing down a fifty pound toddler with knives for knuckles and broken glass for teeth, you might want to pay attention.

Recommended Approach: Sure, most dog owners swear their "Bella" wouldn't hurt a fly. But here's the thing: even the best-behaved dog can bite out of fear or feel threatened if you approach them too quickly. Don't be fooled by the "he doesn't bite" mantra; always err on the side of caution. (Search "Dusty Slay he won't bite". It's hilarious.)

Before diving in for a doggy cuddle session, watch closely for signs of discomfort. A wrinkled muzzle, teeth-baring, bristled fur, an intense stare, or a rigid, upright tail are all red flags. And yes—while pit bulls and rottweilers are often cited as the most notorious biters, golden retrievers, Labradors, and mixed breeds actually account for a large percentage of bites overall.

Now, for the safe approach:

- Soften your gaze and open your mouth. You want to appear friendly, not menacing.
- Approach at an angle, not directly head-on. This feels less threatening to the dog.
- Take a deep breath and relax your body. Nervous energy can be contagious, so stay calm and collected.
- Offer the back of your hand for sniffing. Let the dog decide if they want to be friends.

- If you encounter an aggressive dog, avoid eye contact and speak softly. Slowly back away and become as uninteresting as possible.
- If attacked, get vertical! Climb on top of a car or scale a tree. You should also use whatever you can as a barrier between you and the dog—like a jacket, purse, or backpack—to create distance.

Yes, dogs are precious creatures, but they deserve respect and understanding. By following these tips, you can ensure that your interactions with furry friends are filled with wags, not stitches.

Your Goal: Dating
The Risk: Depression; Financial Loss; Disease; Heartache

THE LESSON: BUILD MEANINGFUL RELATIONSHIPS

Common Mistakes: Diving headfirst into a relationship, online or in person can be exciting and risky. It's during this vulnerable phase that you're most susceptible to scams, unwanted diseases, and a whole lot of regret. Good people are getting scammed and blackmailed on dating apps every day.

Dating fraud is booming, with lovestruck victims losing an average of $2,400 each. And guess what? Real-life dating isn't much better. If things get intimate quickly chances are you'll need a doctor's visit sooner rather than later. The CDC estimates that one in five adults carry the herpes simplex virus (HSV), with no cure in sight. Scary, right? Let's take a step back and approach dating with a clear head.

Recommended Approach: Dating is an amazing journey! We all crave emotional connections with others. But before you rush head-first into the next "perfect" match, embrace this time to explore and grow. Date multiple people, practice genuine communication, and hone your ability to read and relate to different personalities. These basic skills will serve you well in building meaningful connections.

Here's your first rule: prioritize face-to-face meetings. If you met your *new* love interest online, get to a face-to-face as soon as possible. This is the best way to judge the authenticity of the connection.

Take it slow. Even if your best friend introduced you, remember, you don't truly know this person yet. They might not even know themselves! Be open and express your values and opinions, but keep your finances private. Money talk early on is a red flag. True love is selfless, so beware of those who constantly ask for favors or drain you with their drama. You deserve a partner who prioritizes your happiness, just as you do theirs.

Finally, remember this: sending explicit photos is rarely a good idea. It's a major source of blackmail, shame, and regret. Your future self will thank you for skipping the sexting.

So, take your time, explore your options, and prioritize genuine connection over fleeting excitement. Mama knows best on this one: love is a marathon, not a sprint.

Your Goal: Muscle Fitness
The Risk: Neck Pain; Joint Problems; Torn Muscles &
Ligaments, Getting Tiny While Recuperating

THE LESSON: NO PAIN, NO PAIN

Common Mistakes: Hitting the gym with good intentions
but neglecting the resident trainer, is a common mistake. Did
you know that a whopping 18% of gym goers end up injured
while exercising? Ouch! And guess what? Free weights are the

culprit behind most of those injuries. To add insult to injury, young adults between 16 and 25 are twice as likely to get hurt than their exercising parents. Injuries disrupt your workout routine, kill motivation, and, frankly, suck. But fear not, fitness enthusiast! We've got your back (and knees) with these tips to keep you in the game for life.

Recommended Approach: No matter what your fitness goals, focus on four key elements: warming up, proper form, hydration, and variety. A quick five to ten minutes of light cardio like cycling, jogging, or jumping jacks gets your blood flowing and warms up your muscles and joints.

Free weights might seem cool, but the truth is, muscles don't have eyes. Machines are just as effective for most goals, and they offer the added benefit of guiding you into proper form — minimizing injury risk. Steer clear of high-risk exercises like behind-the-neck pulldowns or presses, and avoid deadlifts unless you have impeccable form.

To prevent overuse injuries, particularly in your shoulders and knees, keep your routine fresh and varied. Consider splitting your workouts by muscle groups, dedicating specific days to chest and triceps, biceps and back, and legs. This allows muscles to rest, repair, and grow.

Of course, staying hydrated and fueling your body with proper nutrition and basic supplements are essential for optimal performance. Hey, you're looking proper fit, Bro!

Your Goal: Jogging
The Risk: Stress Fractures; Pain; Assault; Horror Show

THE LESSON: RUN THE SAFE & HEALTHY WAY

Common Mistakes: Jogging has exploded in popularity worldwide, thanks to its affordability and accessibility. The benefits are undeniable: improved overall health, better sleep, enhanced mental well-being, and even a longer lifespan. However, the harsh reality is that roughly 50% of joggers suffer injuries annually. Adding insult to injury, a staggering 85% of female joggers report experiencing harassment or assault during their runs. While the benefits of jogging outweigh the risks, let's explore ways to keep you safe and thriving on your running journey.

Recommended Approach: Forget about meticulously tracking miles and kilometers; it's a trap that often leads to fatigue, injury, and unrealistic expectations. Instead, focus on two key metrics: heart rate and time.

First, we need to determine your target heart rate - the sweet spot for optimal training. To calculate this, subtract your age from 220 and then multiply by 0.75. For example, if you're 22 years old, your target heart rate is 148 beats per minute (220 - 22 = 198, 198 x 0.75 = 148).

Now, the magic happens. Start by walking or alternating between walking and jogging until you reach your target heart rate of 148. Aim to maintain this heart rate for 30 minutes. Repeat this routine 4-5 times a week. As you stick with this plan, your heart, legs, feet, and cardiovascular system will adapt, improve, and gradually demand more intensity over time. Don't be tempted to push yourself too hard; slow and steady wins the race, and you'll be crushing your goals in no time.

While some swear by barefoot running, the jury is still out on the ideal footwear. I recommend keeping it simple: opt for shoes with minimal cushioning to encourage a more natural gait. Finally, let's address the safety concerns, especially for female runners. While every slasher movie seems to prey on the solo jogger, it's not all doom and gloom. If you find yourself without a running buddy or prefer the peace of solo runs, consider these tips:

- Avoid headphones: Stay aware of your surroundings to be alert to potential dangers, many of which your ears were designed to pick up!
- Run during daylight hours: Opt for well-lit areas with plenty of foot traffic and easy escape routes.
- Wear reflective clothing: Increase your visibility to motorists and pedestrians.
- Carry a personal safety device: Please carry a whistle, pepper spray, a stun gun, personal alarm or samurai sword for added peace of mind.

By embracing these simple tips, you can ditch the pain and embrace the joy of running, reaping all the benefits this amazing activity has to offer. Happy jogging!

BUT WAIT, THERE'S MORE!

Based on available data on preventable injuries and deaths in the U.S., I'm quite confident that we addressed most situations you may run into. But not all!

I'm sure I missed some precarious situations, events, and experiences that didn't make this list. That's the beauty of living! We constantly need to adapt to our environment to survive and thrive. Do you have some tips that I should consider for future versions? Are there risks that you want to warn others about? Let's keep the conversation going and, who knows, maybe we can save a life together.

Send me your comments, suggestions and recommendations! I read every one. Email **bergeracpublishing@gmail.com** and **www.bergeracpublishing.com**.

AUTHOR

Introducing Joseph Berger, a career health care executive who debuted as an author with the first edition of "Think Mortally!: A Survival Guide for Young Adults." With an MBA and expertise in marketing and behavioral economics, Joe draws inspiration from his two sons to offer practical life advice in a light, humorous, and direct tone. Based near Philadelphia, Pennsylvania, his mission is to equip young adults with essential skills for a safer, brighter and prosperous future.

BIBLIOGRAPHY

National Safety Council. (2021). "Deaths by Age and Cause." Injury Facts.

National Safety Council. (2021). "Top 10 Preventable Injuries 2021."

National Safety Council. (2021). "All Injuries Overview." Injury Facts.

Hafner, M., Stepanek, M., Taylor, J., Troxel, W. M., & Van Stolk, C. (2016). "Why sleep matters — the economic costs of insufficient sleep: A cross-country comparative analysis." RAND Corporation.

Centers for Disease Control and Prevention. (n.d.). "Sleep Deprivation, Sleep Disorders, and Chronic Disease."

Centers for Disease Control and Prevention. (n.d.). "Sleep and Sleep Disorders."

Centers for Disease Control and Prevention. (2017). "Short Sleep Duration by Occupation Group."

U.S. Fire Administration. "Candle Fire Safety." FEMA. Last reviewed April 1, 2023.

National Safety Council. "State Overview." Injury Facts.

Eadie Hill Trial Lawyers. "Choking and Suffocation Deaths." Eadie Hill Trial Lawyers - Nursing Home Abuse and Neglect Attorneys. Eadie Hill Trial Lawyers.

Chang, A., Schnall, A. H., Law, R., et al. (2020). "Cleaning and Disinfectant Chemical Exposures and Temporal Associations with COVID-19 — National Poison Data System, United States, January 1, 2020–March 31, 2020." MMWR Morb Mortal Wkly Rep, 69, 496–498. Centers for Disease Control and Prevention.

Healthcare Purchasing News. (2020, April 27). "CDC releases report on increased poison cases due to disinfectant chemical exposures with COVID-19." Healthcare Purchasing News.

Stevens, J. A., Haas, E. N., Haileyesus, T. (2008). "Nonfatal Bathroom Injuries Among Persons Aged ≥15 Years — United States." Centers for Disease Control and Prevention.

Thompson Creek. "Safety Stats for Your Bathroom." Thompson Creek.

Shower Bay. "Bathroom Slips And Falls Are Top Causes Of Injuries For The Elderly."

Cullan & Cullan LLC. (2015, May 11). "May Is National Electrical Safety Month: Do You Know the Facts?" Cullan Law.

Nickle Electrical Companies. "Electrical Safety Statistics."

Centers for Disease Control and Prevention. "Estimates of Foodborne Illness in the United States." CDC, 2018.

U.S. Department of Health & Human Services. "Food Poisoning." FoodSafety.gov, 2020.

Smith, G. A. (2013). "Knife-related injuries treated in United States emergency departments, 1990-2008." Journal of Emergency Medicine, 45(3), 315-323. doi: https://doi.org10.1016/j.jemermed.2012.11.092 . Available at: PubMed.

Beaumont Emergency Hospital. "Kitchen Accidents." Available at: Beaumont Emergency Hospital - Kitchen Accidents.

U.S. Food and Drug Administration. "Microwave Ovens." FDA.

Food Safety and Inspection Service. "Cooking with Microwave Ovens." U.S. Department of Agriculture.

Food Creeks. "14 Important Microwave Cooking Safety Tips." Food Creeks.

Zwilling J. A. Henckels: How to Care and Maintain for your Cookware

Tufts Health & Nutrition Letter. (2021). Recognizing the Health Dangers of Ultraprocessed Foods. [online] Available at: www.nutritionletter.tufts.edu

National Highway Traffic Safety Administration. (2021). Distracted Driving Dangers and Statistics.

Centers for Disease Control and Prevention. (2022). Distracted Driving.

Insurance Information Institute. (2024). Facts + Statistics: Distracted driving.

Consumer Affairs Research Team. (2024). Road Rage Statistics 2024. Consumer Affairs. https://www.consumeraffairs.com/news/road-rage-statistics.html.

Berry, L. (2023). Understanding The Impact Of Road Rage: Statistics And Facts In 2023. Obrella. Available at: https://www.obrella.com/auto-insurance/auto-insurance-basics/understanding-the-impact-of-road-rage-statistics-and-facts/.

Consumer Auto. (n.d.). Comprehensive Guide to Car Maintenance: Ensuring Longevity and Optimal Performance. Consumer Auto.

Car Oracle Experts. (2023, December 16). The Lifeblood of Your Car: Understanding the Importance of Regular Oil Changes and Monitoring Oil Levels. Car Oracle

Mayo Clinic Staff. (2022, September 17). Back Pain: Symptoms and Causes. Mayo Clinic. Available at mayoclinic.org

Mayo Clinic Health System. (2021, September 9). Back Pain Self-Care Tips. Mayo Clinic Health System. Available at mayoclinichealthsystem.org

Norwegian News Agency (NTB). (2021, January 25). "Skipping lunch break can be bad to your health." Science Norway. Available at sciencenorway.no.

National Safety Council. "Injury Facts." Available at injuryfacts.nsc.org.

U.S. Bureau of Labor Statistics. (2022). "TABLE A-7. Fatal occupational injuries by worker characteristics and event or exposure, all United States, 2022." Available at bls.gov.

Occupational Safety and Health Administration. "Commonly Used Statistics." Available at osha.gov.

Livestrong.com. "Is It Bad to Drink Alcohol on an Empty Stomach?"

Mayo Clinic. "Hangovers - Symptoms and causes." Available at mayoclinic.org.

LifeHack. "How to Be a Social Success: 7 Secrets." Available at lifehack.org.

SuccessQuest Podcast. "Social Success - Create Meaningful Intentional Relationships." Available at successquest.webflow.io.

National Institute on Alcohol Abuse and Alcoholism (NIAAA). "Understanding Alcohol Use Disorder."

National Institute on Alcohol Abuse and Alcoholism (NIAAA). "Alcohol Use Disorder (AUD) in the United States: Age Groups and Demographic Characteristics."

National Institute on Alcohol Abuse and Alcoholism (NIAAA). "Alcohol Use in the United States: Age Groups and Demographic Characteristics."

World Health Organization. "Radiation: Effects of Ultraviolet (UV) Radiation on the Skin, Eyes and Immune System."

Nature Reviews Immunology. "Photoimmunology: How Ultraviolet Radiation Affects the Immune System." Available at nature.com.

Centers for Disease Control and Prevention. (2023, October 26). Lyme Disease. https://www.cdc.gov/lyme/index.html

National Institutes of Health. (2022, July 19). Lyme Disease. https://www.niaid.nih.gov/diseases-conditions/lyme-disease

American Hiking Society. (2023). Hiking Safety. https://americanhiking.org/

National Park Service. (2023, September 23). Hiking Safety Tips. https://hikingdaily.com/hiking-safety/

Leave No Trace. (2023). Leave No Trace Center for Outdoor Ethics. https://lnt.org/

National Institutes of Health. (2021, May 07). Hiking Safety Tips. https://www.self.com/story/hiking-safety-tips

National Safety Council: https://www.nsc.org/membership/member-resources/injury-facts

Consumer Product Safety Commission: https://www.cpsc.gov/

American Society of Safety Engineers (ASSE): https://www.assp.org/about (Search for "personal protective equipment (PPE)")

Occupational Safety and Health Administration (OSHA): https://www.osha.gov/ (Search for "lawn and landscape")

The Power Tool Institute: https://www.powertoolinstitute.com/

Fact sheet on air pollution and lung health: https://www.lung.org/research/sota/health-risks

Fire safety tips for outdoor fireplaces and fire pits: https://www.seattletimes.com/explore/at-home/outdoor-fireplace-safety-tips/

Statistics on residential fires: https://www.nfpa.org/-/media/files/news-and-research/fire-statistics-and-reports/building-and-life-safety/oshomes.pdf

Fire safety tips for outdoor fireplaces and fire pits: https://www.seattletimes.com/explore/at-home/outdoor-fireplace-safety-tips/

Statistics on residential fires: https://www.nfpa.org/-/media/files/news-and-research/fire-statistics-and-reports/building-and-life-safety/oshomes.pdf

Centers for Disease Control and Prevention (CDC): https://www.cdc.gov/drowning/index.html

The National Drowning Prevention Alliance: https://ndpa.org/

Water safety tips for swimming in national parks: https://www.nps.gov/subjects/oceans/water-safety.htm?msclkid=67e92917ae9a11ec8655a00dce89baf9

Water Education Foundation: https://www.watereducation.org

Florida Smart. (n.d.). Florida Beach Safety Guide: Beach Flags, Rip Currents, Dangerous Sea Life. Available at www.floridasmart.com.

U.S. Department of Commerce. (2022, July 21). Beach Safety and Avoiding Rip Currents: Advice from NOAA.

NOAA's National Ocean Service. (n.d.). Dangers at the Beach. Available at oceanservice.noaa.gov

Sail Magazine. "Meclizine vs. Dramamine: Which Is Better for Sea Sickness?"

Divers Alert Network. "Seasickness Prevention and Treatment." Divers Alert Network (DAN), 4 August 2020.

Reel Coquina Blog. "How to Prevent Seasickness while Fishing." Reel Coquina Blog.

Wikipedia. (2023). "Seoul Halloween crowd crush." https://en.wikipedia.org/wiki/Seoul_Halloween_crowd_crush

Reuters. (2023). "One year after the deadly crowd crush in Seoul." Available at https://www.reuters.com/world/asia-pacific/skorea-installs-cctv-cameras-with-ai-tech-prevent-another-disaster-like-2022-10-24/

Pew Research Center. (2023). "What the data says about gun deaths in the U.S."

Pew Research Center. (2023). "Key facts about Americans and guns."

The Trace. (2023). "Gun Violence in 2022, By the Numbers."

Centers for Disease Control and Prevention. (2023). "Fast Facts: Firearm Violence and Injury Prevention."

Psychology Today. (n.d.). "What Types of People Fall Prey to Scams?"

Routledge. (n.d.). "The Psychology of Fraud, Persuasion and Scam Techniques."

Ferlick, M. (n.d.). "De-Escalation Is a Go-To Tactic for Behavior-Related Incidents." Psychology Today.

DogsBite.org. "U.S. Dog Bite Statistics."

American Veterinary Medical Association. "Dog bite risk and prevention: The role of breed."

Federal Trade Commission. (2022). "Reports of romance scams hit record highs in 2021."

Centers for Disease Control and Prevention. (2021). "Genital Herpes Statistics."

Gitnux. (n.d.). Must-Know Gym Injuries Statistics [Recent Analysis].

Muscle & Brawn. (n.d.). 14 Lifting Injury Statistics (Bodybuilding And Weights).

LIVESTRONG. (2024). 126 Running Statistics You Need to Know in 2024. Available at https://www.livestrong.com

RunRepeat. (2021/2022). 120+ Running Statistics 2021/2022 [Research Review]. Available at https://runrepeat.com

World Athletics. (2021). New Research Reveals Running Boom During Covid-19 Pandemic.

www.ingramcontent.com/pod-product-compliance
Lightning Source LLC
Chambersburg PA
CBHW051309250726
48656CB00004B/1561